Devil's Advocate Economics:
The Other Side of the Stories

Devil's Advocate Economics:
The Other Side of the Stories

Katherine Davis Butler

Econ Books Now
2018

First Printing: 2018

ISBN 978-0-359-20926-2

econbooksnow@gmail.com

Ordering Information:
Special discounts are available on quantity purchases when this book is purchased directly from the distributor lulu.com.

Contents

Introduction

I originally intended this book for a college-aged audience, perhaps even hoping that some professors would adopt the book as reading for their economics courses. I feel this text would certainly be thought-provoking and exciting in that use. But anyone with an interest in economics, politics, or social issues can (and in my humble opinion, should) read this book. You might nod your head in agreement. You might throw down this book in disgust. Maybe you'll do both of those things depending on which pages you're reading.

This isn't just meant to be another trendy book of the newly-created pop-economics publishing trend. There have been books such as The Undercover Economist and the Freakonomics series, publishing thoughtful vignettes about various topics. However, while stories about sumo wrestling and drug dealing street gangs may be interesting, they are likely to have little application or relevance to the everyday reader or student.

This text aims to examine the economics of phenomena and activities that are more likely to be of importance and relevance for a typical reader or student. Further, the book will examine the economics of each topic, and give insights that often fly in the face of existing traditions, biases, and sometimes even political correctness. Politically, parts of this book will likely upset both liberals and conservatives alike.

Having said that, I didn't write this book to be an echo chamber for the political left or right. In fact, the book isn't meant to be overly political. Sure, certain policies and laws will be discussed – but only to illustrate how they affect individual and firm behavior. That is what economics is about – studying the actions of individuals and firms, and seeing how behavior changes when costs, benefits, or incentives are changed. People tend to think that politics and government can solve all problems, ranging from discrimination and inequality to poor education and expensive college tuition. But presidents, politicians, and laws can't fix all the problems we have.

Laws and policies that affect and distort markets are often one-size-fits-all blunt instruments that create winners and losers rather than helping everyone. In addition, bureaucrats and lobbyists often take complex economic issues and present them in a much too simplistic (and sometimes dishonest) way and then present a nice-sounding, but ultimately ineffective, "solution".

My hope is that after reading this book, the reader will
- See that individuals respond to incentives, and that underground or illegal activity is often the result of legal markets not providing the goods people need.
- See that the "problems" which politicians attempt to fix through laws and legislation are often far more nuanced than we think. Further, the proposed "solution" is often too simplified and won't correct the underlying issue.
- Become more logical in their thinking and understanding of news and events, and in their personal decision making.
- Discover and discard some personal or political biases.
- View the world through the lens of an economist.

In Defense of the Rich

In 2016, a New Jersey resident decided to leave the state and move to Florida. This sort of thing happens all the time and would normally be of little or no concern to state lawmakers. However, in this special case, New Jersey officials were panicked about the prospect of this one special person moving away, fearing that his exit would leave the state with a $150 million budget shortfall. How could this be?

+++++++++++++

You see, the person who decided to move away was billionaire David Tepper, who at the time was the owner of Appaloosa Management, an American hedge fund. Here are some numbers: According to the New York Times, Tepper earned more than $6 billion between 2012 and 2015. The highest bracket for state income taxes in New Jersey is 8.97%. New Jersey and Mr. Tepper won't say how much he paid in taxes, but with those numbers it could have been upward of $450 million during those years. Thus, this super-earner paid super-taxes, and his departure could have large ramifications for state coffers. For comparison, Florida does not have a state personal income tax. As a result, relocating to Florida would save Tepper millions of dollars (perhaps billions) over the next decade of his life. The sunny weather isn't the only reason many people choose to spend their retirement in Florida.

On a broader scale, there have been many rallies over the last few years in the name of social justice, inequality, fairness, etc. The standard battle cry at these rallies has been calling out "the 1%" – the very top earners who earn a large portion of the country's income and own a large part of the country's wealth. The call has been that it isn't fair – they don't deserve what they have, they are greedy, they steal money from the poor, and they *certainly* don't pay their fair share in taxes!

Let's look at the "fair share" argument. The word "fair" is certainly a normative (opinion) word. Many people point to the taxes paid by the rich, and point out that on a percentage basis, rich people sometimes pay a smaller percentage of their income in taxes compared to others. This occurs partly because many rich people have earnings from long term capital gains, which are taxed at a lower rate than income taxes. Thus, say the people, this is an unfair system. It exploits the poor, the rich are greedy, etc. But let's examine just the actual numbers. The New York Times stated that Tepper's tax bill in 2013 alone may have been near $300 million. That means that in that one year, he paid multiples more in taxes than you or I will ever pay in our entire lives. He paid more in taxes in that one year than my entire graduation class pays in a decade (unless one of my classmates also secretly became a billionaire). How much more do we want him to pay? He may certainly have more income and wealth than many of us, but do we really expect a very tiny fraction of the population to foot most of the tax bill?

While many people complain about a rich person's personal tax rate, let's examine the *overall* percent of taxes that are paid by the rich. In New Jersey, 40% of the state's budget comes from state income taxes, and just 100 people pay over 5.5% of all income tax payments. That bears repeating. In a state with a population of 8.6 million people, just 100 residents (0.0011% of the population) are responsible for 5.5% of the tax burden. Furthermore, less than 1% of the taxpayers in the state contribute one-third of the total income tax collected. In fact, in at least 5 states (New Jersey, New York, Connecticut, California, and Maryland), the top 1% of earners pay more than one-third of the state's income taxes.

> The top 1% of earners own 17% of the income but pay almost half of federal income taxes.

The phenomenon also exists on the national level. According to a study by the Tax Policy Center, the top 1% of earners owned 17% of income in the United States in 2014, but that same group paid 45.7% (almost half!) of federal income taxes. Looking at those numbers, you could conclude that the tax code is already very progressive and stacked *against* the rich. When you hear people ranting about the top 1%, they'll complain about how much income and wealth the rich have, but they will quietly and conveniently forget to mention the staggering amount of taxes that the super wealthy pay.

Note that this is a different set of numbers from then-presidential-candidate Mitt Romney's infamous "47%" line, where he stated that 47% of Americans pay no income tax. Romney forgot to mention that within that 47%, there are many young people under the age of 18, retired people, and people not in the labor force. Rather, this discussion is about the <u>actual amount</u> of taxes collected. Almost half of the taxes collected come from just 1% of the population. Thus, if/when taxes are reduced, it's only natural (not a conspiracy) that the largest benefactors in absolute terms will be the rich. If everyone's tax bill is reduced by 10%, what happens? Someone who pays no taxes will get nothing back. Some who pays $20,000 a year will get $2,000 back. Tepper will get millions back. Those darn rich people get all the breaks!! (Just remember not tell anyone that those rich people, even after a tax break, continue to pay billions more in taxes than the rest of us combined).

But consider New Jersey again. Residents are faced not only with high state income taxes, but also an estate tax, an inheritance tax, and the country's highest property tax. Can you really blame Tepper for leaving? If most other residents had the means, would they do the same? Going back to the numbers, the estimated shortfall created by Tepper's departure could have been covered by having the 8.6 million people pay an average of just $17.44 each. But you'll certainly imagine the political firestorm that would be created if the state dared to ask all people to pay a tiny bit more because one person got tired of paying $150 million each year.

> If we tax the rich too much, they may just move away, creating a big tax problem for the rest of us.

Is there a lesson to be learned here? Before retirement age, most people can't afford to move to another state simply for tax reasons. But the rich can, and this case certainly shows that they do. If we continually try to soak the rich for more and more tax dollars, they may simply move away. If Tepper found it worthwhile to leave the state, what is to stop the next 99 richest people from moving, and causing a 5.5% reduction in New Jersey state funds? This case certainly provides strong evidence for a downward-sloping portion of the Laffer Curve.

You can continue to call the rich evil, selfish, and greedy if you must. I know that I would certainly move from New Jersey to Florida if doing so would save me $150 million per year. You would too.

The Gender Wage Gap: Fact or Myth?

"For every dollar a man earns, a woman earns 75 cents". You've heard that phrase before. I guarantee you'll hear it again. You have heard it (or will hear it) in some of your college courses. You'll hear the phrase mindlessly parroted by journalists, lobbyists, politicians, and social justice warriors.

With so many people repeating this phrase, it must be true!

Right?

Like so many "facts" and "statistics" that people tend to repeat thoughtlessly, we'll see that this is far more nuanced. Could this statement be a *little bit* misleading? Or maybe even extremely misleading? Maybe even downright false? Do the people that repeat the phrase ad nauseum even know where it comes from, or what data is used to get the result?

"For every dollar a man earns, a woman earns 75 cents". This is almost universally referred to as the **gender wage gap**. But this phrase in its familiar form is extremely misleading at best. At worst, it is an intentionally misrepresented lie.

Let's examine this statement.

++++++++++++++

The gender wage gap is almost always presented to society in the following simplistic (and incorrect) way: Men make more than women, and the sole cause is discrimination. Employers are intentionally paying women 25% less just because of their gender. We must fight this discrimination by passing legislation, making women a protected class, and requiring equal pay for equal work.

The gender wage gap statistic neglects to include even a single variable that causes wage differences among people. It doesn't even account for job differences!

The main problem with the wage gap statement is where the numbers come from. The statement comes from simply comparing the average earnings of all men and women. This shows the women earn 25% less on average. Discrimination must be the cause! Well, no. The statistic only accounts for wage and gender. It does not account for education differences. It does not account for differences in hours worked. It does not account for how many years people have been working, or how much time they've taken off. Most importantly, this "statistic" (sarcastic quotes) doesn't even account for job differences! In other words, it compares neurosurgeons to nurses. It compares superintendents to recess supervisors. This is a terrible way to make any comparison, and in fact makes any attempt to compare wages meaningless.

Here is an example: Suppose a male CEO in New York City has a Master's degree and has operated his company for 20 years. There is also a female social worker in South Dakota. She has an Associate's degree, works part time, and is in her first year on the job. Who would you predict has higher earnings? The male. Is this gender discrimination? Common sense says no – the male is a CEO, lives in a big city, and has more experience and education. However, the wage gap statistic ignores all of that. It only looks at two things – wage and gender. And if a male earns more than a female, it is implicitly assumed to be due to gender discrimination since no other factors are even examined. Hopefully now you can see why I and many economists call the gender wage gap statistic very misleading, if not downright dishonest.

Economists have studied the wage gap extensively. They find that many non-discrimination factors account for most of the wage gap.

First and foremost are job differences. Restating the obvious, not all jobs pay the same. But why? Some jobs require more education and more skills. Some jobs require longer working hours. Some jobs require working in unpleasant or dangerous conditions. Some jobs require prolonged travel. There are many other factors. These are all referred to as **compensating wage differentials**. If you want to hire someone with more education, you have to pay them more because their opportunity cost of working for you is higher (they lose out on more pay from not taking other jobs). Further, if you want someone to work in any condition that could not be considered ideal, you must compensate them for it. Even though a high school custodian and coal miner might have the same education and weekly hours, the coal miner will likely get paid more since the job is more dangerous. As another example, consider an oil rig. Jobs on the rig require prolonged absences from home. Shifts are long and dangerous. If you make a mistake, you could cause an oil spill or death (either your own or a coworker's). As such, these conditions require higher pay to attract workers. And most workers on the rig are men. Why is this? Maybe men are more willing to take jobs that have these risks, to some extent valuing high pay over safety and comfort. It isn't sexist to point this out. Men and women might just have different preferences and risk tolerances for certain activities.

Jobs clearly have pay differences. But we also see that genders are not equally distributed across all jobs. Men tend to be over-represented in jobs that have higher pay, but they are also much more likely to die or get injured on the job. Women tend to be over-represented in jobs that have lower pay, but they are more likely to be in jobs where they can enjoy flexible hours or more comfortable working conditions. Once again, this isn't sexism. It is just an aggregation of revealed preferences of men and women.

Some people view the fact that not all jobs are 50% men and 50% women and call it discrimination. But it's not. It isn't possible (and isn't ethical) to use laws, quotas, or social engineering to make sure that all jobs have equal numbers of men and women employed. Perhaps this will change organically over time for some higher-paying jobs over the next couple of decades as we are already seeing women outnumber men in college. This will certainly reduce differences in the average pay of men and women, but education is just one factor.

Even if we have an ideal experiment setting where we find a job that is done by exactly the same number of men and women with the exact same education, there still may be pay differences that aren't discriminatory. Numerous studies have found that even in full-time jobs, men tend to work longer hours and take less time off than women. One reason for this is family – when child care or elder care is needed, women are more likely than men to take prolonged absences from the labor force. This reduces job tenure and promotion opportunities. But once again, this is not discrimination and legislation can't fix it. You can't legislate for more men to stay home and take care of family as an attempt to eliminate the wage gap. It would also be extreme legislative overreach to try to punish firms that consider time absent from work when examining who to promote.

There is also an important factor that is often overlooked. Many employers aren't just walking around giving raises beyond a standardized amount each year. If you want a pay raise or promotion, you usually have to ask for it. Many studies have found that men simply ask for raises more often. This begins even before the job starts. Women are more likely to accept the original salary offer while men are more likely to use the starting offer as the beginning of a negotiation.

Rather than looking at all the nuances and real factors that cause the gender wage gap, politicians and lobbyists just find it easier and more convenient to blame it on discrimination.

Maybe I've convinced you that most of the gender wage gap is NOT discrimination. At this point, we have to ask ourselves about the people (politicians, lobbyists, social justice warriors) who love repeating the gender wage gap statement. Are they really ignorant about the data, or are they just being purposefully dishonest? With many social justice warriors, we could assume the former as they are likely just parroting talking points they've heard from others rather than doing any meaningful reading and research about the subject on their own. But with politicians and lobbyists, we can't be as certain. We would like to at least *hope* that politicians, running for some of the highest offices in our country, would be well-informed, honest, and not purposefully misleading (I hear you laughing now). But with politics comes the need for votes. Support is more likely to come if the politician can create an easy rallying cry for voters, and discrimination is an easy boogeyman on which to place blame. Thus, many politicians of the last three decades have used the trope of "you're a victim of the system, you're being oppressed by discrimination, and I'm the person to solve this problem". And voters (maybe we're just lazy), seem to eat this up. I suspect that many politicians have taken at least some classes in economics, labor relations, or business, and are aware of the nuances and non-discrimination factors that cause differences in the average earnings of men and women. But it isn't easy (and certainly isn't popular) to talk about those. It's just much easier to blame it on discrimination, and then claim that you, as an elected official, will legislate and force the discrimination to go away. And millions of voters will somehow believe you.

Finally, we could attempt to answer the question about why men are overrepresented in higher paying jobs and women are overrepresented in lower paying jobs. Part of this could have to do with preferences – men might be happier to work alone, in high-stress jobs, or with machines rather than people. Women might prefer to work with others and have flexible hours. These preferences could certainly steer job choice. If these really are the choices made by men and women of their own volition, we shouldn't try to legislate against that. Otherwise, we step toward the terrible scenario of having gender quotas in jobs simply to try to equalize average pay.

But interestingly, there could be some events that occur long before the job market that might shape these preferences. Maybe men were more likely than women to be given building blocks and robotic toys as kids. Maybe women were more likely to be given dolls and stuffed animals as kids. This in turn could result in more men becoming interested in engineering (high paying jobs) and more women to be interested in nursing or teaching (lower paying jobs). If true, this could certainly affect average earnings of men and women by contributing to men being over-represented in high-paying jobs and women being over-represented in low-paying jobs. This is why there has been a large push to get young girls interested in STEM programs. There are many all-girl camps, retreats, and events to help achieve the goal of getting more women employed in the sciences and engineering. But we must be careful not to leave boys behind – remember that they are already outnumbered in college.

Equal Pay for Equal Work

Now a short addendum. Perhaps I've convinced you that the gender wage gap is largely caused by job differences rather than discrimination. Although I fully realize that some lobbyists, politicians, and sociologists will never agree with that.

I'd still be in favor of "equal pay for equal work" though... Or not? Well, sit down and prepare to perhaps be disappointed again.

+++++++++++++

"Equal pay for equal work" is another phrase that sounds nice. It sounds like something we should be striving for without exception. Equal Pay is an issue that almost always gets tied to gender, but no one seems to complain when two people of the same gender have different pay within a firm. But once again, there are many nuances here.

First and foremost, "equal work" is often not a realistic comparison to make. Even if two people are in the same business with the same title, there can be many differences. For example, one person may have more education, a different degree, or even a degree from a different school. One person may work longer hours within the job or have taken few days off. Someone may have been at the company a year or two longer. Shouldn't those factors allow for pay differences, even if there is "equal work"?

Fine, you say. We can pay people more if they have more job tenure, education, or put in longer hours. But if we can find two people with identical characteristics and identical performance in the job, they should get the same pay!! Even then, I say no. Any sort of legislation on how much firms must pay their employees will have serious unintended consequences.

One thing that employers (and employees) consider regarding salary is the opportunity cost of the employee. What could they be doing elsewhere? In other words, what *other* potential job (and salary) is the employee giving up in order to take *this* job? On a related note, what was the previous salary before this job? Did the employee take a pay raise or pay cut with this new job compared to the previous job?

Consider two people, Alice and Bob, both stars in the field of consulting. They have both been recently hired at Beantown Consulting in Boston, with Bob being hired just one week after Alice. They will work together daily as a team on projects. They both had 5 years previous work experience in consulting. They both graduated Magna Cum Laude in the same year from North Carolina State, each with a degree in Economics. Yet, Bob earns a salary of $130,000, and Alice earns a salary of $110,000. Is this discrimination? Is Beantown paying Bob a huge amount more just because he is a man? Most likely not. There are still some pieces of information missing: What were the previous salaries of Bob and Alice? Where were their previous jobs?

Even if two people are at the same firm doing the same job, pay differences may exist due to differing salaries at previous jobs. All other things equal, most people are not willing to take a pay cut at a new job.

For the previous 5 years, Alice had been working at Cape View consulting, also located in Boston. Her salary was $94,000 at Cape View, but there had been some difficulties. There had been a lot of turnover at the company, and she didn't like her boss very well. When some job vacancies were posted at Beantown, she decided to apply. Beantown offered her a position with a $110,000 salary. An opportunity for a new job in the same city, with better people, a better boss, *and* higher pay! Alice immediately and graciously accepted. She was happy to start right away.

Now to Bob. For the previous 5 years, Bob had been working at Cloudy Sky consulting, located in Seattle. His salary was $115,000 at Cloudy Sky. Bob generally liked his job, and he had family in the Seattle area. However, he felt like he had reached his peak at Cloudy Sky and decided to see what would happen if he applied to other jobs. Like Alice, Bob applied for a position at Beantown. However, Bob negotiated a salary of $130,000. He was already earning $115,000 in Seattle, so in order to take a new job, move across the country, and leave the proximity of family, a salary increase was necessary for him to justify the change. The salary was agreed upon by both parties, and Bob started his new job at Beantown in Boston.

Thus, we ended up in a situation where two people doing equal work are not receiving equal pay. Is this discrimination? No, it is not. The pay difference isn't because of gender differences or discrimination. If Beantown wanted to hire Bob, they *had* to pay him more because his previous salary was higher. Most people will not willingly take a pay cut for a new job. He also had to move across the country. However, at first glance, only knowing the salaries of Alice and Bob, many readers would just instantly assume gender discrimination and cry foul, or lead an "equal pay" protest against Beantown.

Let's imagine the same story now, but ask what would happen if Equal Pay laws were strictly enforced in all possible ways, requiring Bob and Alice to receive the same salary at Beantown. There are two possible results. The first is that Bob never gets hired. When Beantown tells him they are only legally allowed to pay him $110,000 (the figure that Alice accepted), he will simply decline the job offer. He is not willing to move across the country to take a pay cut.

The second is that Beantown decides that they *really* want or need Bob. Thus, they honor his $130,000 salary request. However, they are now legally required to pay Alice $130,000. Does Alice deserve a $20,000 pay raise, after one week of work, just because the firm hired Bob? The cost of hiring Bob now is at least $150,000 per year – his pay plus Alice's pay raise. The firm may even have to pay other people in the same position more to match Bob's salary, making Bob's hire even more costly.

You can see that the first scenario is much more likely than the second. Bob would just never get hired. Thus, Equal Pay laws didn't help Alice. They just hurt Bob (and possibly Beantown since they didn't hire an experienced worker).

You can see we have an example of a policy meant to make things "fair", but rather ends up hurting people. It is also quick to see another very large flaw with Equal Pay laws. Equal Pay law won't bring *up* everyone's pay to the highest. It is more likely to bring *down* everyone's pay to the lowest. Alternatively, these laws may simply cause firms to underpromote higher earners and overpromote lower earners in an effort to equalize pay, with no regards to other factors. This may cause harder workers and longer-tenured employees to leave the company, and ultimately hurt everyone.

> Equal Pay law doesn't empower workers. It instead takes away the ability of a worker to negotiate for a higher pay. This results in the law creating a wage ceiling rather than helping workers. Salaries will be dropped to the lowest employee's pay to equalize salaries.

California and New York City have recently passed legislation that makes it illegal for an employer to ask about a potential employee's prior salary during the hiring process. The intention, once again, was to try to make things fair and equalize pay. But this will cause many problems, including those already mentioned. Job listings often don't list a specific salary. Sometimes a range is given, or it is stated that salary is commensurate with experience. But if an employer can't know your past salary, they have no idea what to offer to match or beat it. Thus, the entire interview process could be a waste of everyone's time and money. It would be much more efficient if all numbers were shown and given up front, and parties could decide if the interview and visit was worth doing in the first place.

Further, Equal Pay, even if zealously enforced, can only work within one firm. Unless there is a massive increase in government power and control, we can't legally mandate that all consulting firms across the country pay the same salaries. Thus, another undesired consequence would be a decrease in labor mobility across firms. Suppose Firm X has equal pay pegged at $80,000 for all junior associates and Firm Y has equal pay pegged at $84,000. In this case, Firm X would never be able to hire anyone from Firm Y. It would either mean a pay cut for the hired employee (which he would not accept), or Firm X would have to give all of their existing employees a $4,000 raise, at minimum, just to hire the new person.

Finally, Equal Pay enforcement won't empower employees. In fact, it will take away any power they have to negotiate higher salaries. The firm can simply (and truthfully) say "Sorry, I can't pay you more. It's illegal". Thus, the Equal Pay becomes a wage ceiling! This is certainly another example of a large unintended consequence (economic irony, if you will). A nice-sounding policy with the goal of helping people ends up hurting them. This seems to happen a lot, and you'll find many more examples of this the more you study economics and public policy.

Fairness and Wages

Policies regarding wages are often based on notions of fairness. The problem is that fairness means different things to different people. One person may think it's only fair for everyone to get paid the same. Others may think it's unfair to force everyone to the same salary.

People place a high value on fairness. But once again, it fallacious to assume that pay differences are due to discrimination or some other unfair reason.

+++++++++++++++

Consider Alice and Bob again. Suppose Alice was extremely happy with her new $110,000 salary. She celebrated with friends, called her parents, and felt great. Then, she finds out that Bob is making $130,000. Rationally, this shouldn't affect Alice. She is still making more than her previous job. Her money still buys more than her previous salary. Bob's income should in no way affect her work ability or the way she spends her income. But humans are very concerned about fairness. Alice doesn't like the fact that Bob is earning more than her, even though she knows his pay has no effect on her life. She doesn't feel as happy now, even with the higher pay.

Both high and low income workers have notions of fairness.

There are many studies in behavioral economics and psychology that show how much people value fairness. Consider the "Ultimatum Game", with Player A and Player B. Player A is given a sum of money, and he chooses how to split it between himself and Player B. Player B is then asked to accept or reject the split. If Player B accepts, both players get the money according to the split decided by Player A. If Player B rejects, both players get nothing. Many experiments have shown that Player B consistently rejects splits seen as very unfair, even though it results in him getting nothing. Player B willingly sacrifices a positive payoff to prevent an unfair ending where someone else gets more. He would rather have both players get nothing than have the other player end with much more than him. This could be seen as irrational, but it shows empirically that humans place a large value on perceived fairness of outcomes.

But high earners value fairness as well. Many people who put in the time, effort, tenure, and education to earn a high salary will think it is quite unfair if others with less experience and education earn the same salary they do.

Consider the case of Dan Price, CEO of a company called Gravity Payments. After a hostile encounter with an employee who accused Price of ripping him off, Price decided that the minimum salary at his company would be $70,000. This sounds amazing – everyone would be better, and that salary is just so much more "fair" to workers! But there were problems, and many didn't see it as fair. Two of his most experienced and highest level (and higher paid) employees soon quit. Despite their skill and job tenure, they got no raises since they were above the $70,000 minimum. But people at Gravity with much less skill and job tenure were getting $40,000 raises. That's sure to upset most people – seeing someone with less

Even if a colleague earns more than you, your income is still worth the same. Focus on your income, your bills, and your life rather than what someone else is earning. Their money doesn't affect you.

experience getting a 100% raise while you get nothing. Further, Price's brother (and partial owner of Gravity) sued him, alleging that Price was paid too much to begin with and that the large wage change was just for selfish publicity and would reduce firm profitability.

An interesting lesson is learned here. If you try to artificially inflate the wages of lower-skilled and less tenured people, you may just end up losing your higher skilled workers. Perceptions of fairness matter to everyone – not just those with lower incomes.

Comedian George Carlin famously said "Have you ever noticed when you're driving that anyone who's driving slower than you is an idiot, and anyone driving faster than you is a maniac?" People, concerned with fairness, often think in a similar way about income and wealth. We are often guilty of having the following narrative in our heads: "Anyone who has less money than me is lazy and unmotivated. They deserve their financial troubles. Anyone who has more money than me got their money by cheating, taking advantage of others, or just inheriting their wealth. How greedy of them!" Often, neither one of those stereotypes is entirely true. But we have these feelings because we are extremely concerned about fairness. Perhaps it's just part of human nature.

Envy is a tough emotion to deal with – but it may help to realize that your rich neighbor/friend/colleague is just one person. He may have more than you – but his wealth does not affect what you have nor what you can get. If you make $50,000 per year, don't get mad if your coworker earns $55,000 per year. As stated earlier, there may be a number of reasons why he earns more. But the important thing is that his extra money didn't take away anything from you. Your money is still worth the same. If you want to earn more, go and get that raise.

Equality and Poverty

The previous readings on wage differences might also get you to think about wealth. Remember there is a difference between income and wealth. Income is your yearly earnings. Wealth is your accumulated net worth, including assets and savings. Thus, economists, politicians, lobbyists, academics, and anyone else interested in the topics can talk both about income gaps and wealth gaps. This is often done with the intention of discussing discrimination, which may or may not be the real cause of wealth and income gaps.

With talk of wealth and income inequality comes talk of redistribution policy.

+++++++++++++

Redistribution involves methods of legally taking money from high wealth individuals and passing it to low wealth individuals. Some ideas sound good to the average person. But many are downright bad ideas. It is tempting to ask why we can't just take money from the hyper-rich forcefully, and give it to others. Consider the information below with the net worth of some mega-rich people in mid-2018:

- Warren Buffet (Berkshire Hathaway): $89 billion
- Mark Zuckerberg (Facebook): $61 billion
- Bill Gates (Microsoft): $97 billion
- Jeff Bezos (Amazon): $163 billion

Why can't we just take all of the money from these people and give it to charity or use it to fund public services? We could even let them all keep $1 billion, which should be more than enough for any person! Think of all the schools, hospitals, and roads that could be built or fixed! Think of how many children could be given a free lunch at school every day for decades to come!

I admit, I used to think this. Sometimes, it can even be hard to not fall back into that thinking when you see the extremely large net worth of some people. But just arbitrarily picking a wealth ceiling and taxing 100% above it is problematic.

It is tempting to ask why we can't just take forcibly take away most of the wealth from billionaires. Couldn't we spend that money on public services and help many people?

First, these people don't have billions of physical dollars in a safe or even in a checking account. Most of their worth is in their companies that they founded and own. Taking away this wealth would be taking away their business. A business that they built! We don't want to punish success.

Further, if we just forced them to sell their stock shares, they would lose control of their business. In addition, the sale of hundreds of thousands of shares would cause the stock price to fall, hurting anyone who invested in that company.

That situation must seem extreme. Surely no one (at least no one with any influence) is seriously advocating for forcefully taking most of the property and wealth away that is owned by the rich…

Actually, this is a very real scenario.

In 2018, South African president Cyril Ramaphosa stated that no farmer should own more than 20,000 acres of land. This created a fear of land expropriation, in which land would be forcefully taken away, without compensation. As a result, large landowners quickly tried to sell huge amounts of land, and some even fled the country. After all, it's better to sell your land than have it taken away. The huge amounts of land for sale on the market caused land prices to crash, hurting all landowners, not just wealthy ones.

Ramaphosa's policy had racial undertones, as most of the large landowners were white. But the larger issue is that forcefully removing land or other assets eliminates property rights and destroys individual freedoms. If land is allowed to be expropriated, what assets will the government seize next? A very terrible precedent is sent.

Speaking of precedents, we do have a precedent of this happening before, in the country of Zimbabwe. The result of the expropriation was a ruined economy and hyperinflation. But the South African president claimed he learned from others' mistakes, and that South Africa was not going to be a repeat of Zimbabwe.

Attacking property rights may very well be the quickest way to bring economic growth to a halt. It is not surprising that people, both rich and poor, want to be able to keep what they earn. This is why people work hard, take risks, start businesses, and try to invent new goods or technology. It is all about incentives. If uncertainty arises in which the government might just be able to take your assets, patents, or wealth, the incentive to work hard is removed. Why work hard if the government can take my profits? Why put in time and effort if I can't keep my own business? Thus, productivity slows as well as economic growth. Strong property rights are the foundation for keeping an economy growing. Property rights give the incentive for people to be productive.

> Putting property rights in jeopardy and forcibly taking private property removes the incentive for individuals to work hard and take risks. It is a fast way to stop economic growth and ruin an economy.

Back to America now. We understand there are productivity differences in people, but we still might think it is unfair that some people have more wealth than they could spend in 100 lifetimes. And these feelings of unfairness are often the drivers of policy to reduce the wealth of the rich. We think we'd be better off if the rich didn't have so much money and we were just a bit more equal. If taking away large sums of money from the rich would make the rest of us better off, we can consider a day you all should certainly remember – July 26th, 2018. That day, the price of Facebook shares fell 25%. Mark Zuckerberg lost 16.8 <u>billion</u> dollars in a single day. After that day, we were all certainly more equal with Zuckerberg as the gap between his wealth and ours was greatly reduced. But were we better off? Not at all. "But that's because <u>we</u> didn't get that money", you say! This loss of wealth went to no one since it was just share prices that fell. But suppose we could have orchestrated this large decrease in Zuckerberg's wealth to our benefit. We could forcefully confiscate and liquidate his holdings and distribute the $16.8 billion to all Americans. Sadly, we all only get $50 each. Thus, we have wiped out 25% of very rich person's wealth, just so we could all get a free tank of gas. Is this tank of gas really worth stealing a huge amount of a business and the CEO's wealth? Is it worth destroying our institutions of private property rights in the process?

Ultimately, many of the mega-wealthy have pledged to donate much of their fortunes to charity. What the charities will do with this money is yet to be seen, but I think we can all hope it will be something to benefit all of mankind. But the important part of this is that they **chose** to donate. They were not forced or compelled by law.

Don't Exchange Gifts at Christmas

You may of course be familiar with the phrase "Tis better to give than receive". Oddly enough, this could be true in a manner completely unintended by the original spirit of the phrase.

+++++++++++++

In your studying of economics, you may have become familiar with some concepts such as gains from trade, and maybe even deadweight loss. Gains from trade are the result of a consumer paying $15 for something she values at $20. She is $5 better off as a result of the trade. The seller had $11 worth of costs in the production of the good but sold it for $15. The seller is $4 better off. Thus, the trade resulted in both the buyer and the seller experiencing gains.

Deadweight loss might not be discussed as often, but it can arise because of taxes, market frictions, or non-competitive markets, all of which could cause potential beneficial trades to not occur. This creates foregone opportunities for gain. Consumers and producers could have been better. This is called economic inefficiency, and it implies that gains from trade are not maximized.

So where do Christmas gifts fit into this? Well, a gift is just that – a gift. You receive it from a friend or family member rather than buying it for yourself. Also, many gifts are surprises – you don't know what you're going to get until you open it.

This surprise gift you receive may be valuable to you. But it might not be. Thus, an interesting comparison is to be made: How much does the recipient value the gift? How much did the giver pay for it? This is still a cost-benefit comparison of sorts. An interesting result can happen if the recipient values the gift at a smaller amount than the giver paid for it. Imagine you receive a large, heavy, sculpture from an art aficionado friend. You have no clue what the sculpture is, and think it even looks a little inappropriate, but you still graciously accept the gift. You personally value the sculpture at $20 – that would be the most you'd pay for this thing. But your friend paid $300 for it. Considering just these two numbers, you'll see that the cost of this gift is greater than the benefit. This is another example of how deadweight loss and inefficiency can enter into a market – when actions were taken in which costs were greater than benefits.

It is common for gift recipients to feel lukewarm about gifts. You've probably experienced this feeling yourself a time or two.

So if the recipient is often not really impressed or pleased with gifts, why give? Because there are benefits to giving. This could include the joy of watching a friend open a gift or just the good feelings associated with giving. Further, (depending on the exact nature of the social setting) the giver of an expensive gift may gain social standing among friends as a result of showing off their wealth. In certain cases, such

> If a friend buys you a $300 gift that you only value at $20, a net loss to society has occurred. This is economic inefficiency.

as a fancy wine or art club, the gift giver may even think they benefit even more by giving obscure and useless gifts in an effort to appear more elite, sophisticated, or snobby. Thus, for many reasons, it is possible that the gift giver values the act of giving more than the receiver values the gift.

What's the better alternative to giving gifts? One solution would be to give gift cards to the recipient's favorite restaurant or store. This would be more useful to them since they could buy goods they wanted, but it risks the giver looking cheap or thoughtless. But even gift cards have issues – they can only be used at certain places (or even certain times), and thus come with extra transaction costs for the recipient. A better gift would be just to give money, or even a lottery ticket. Money is sure a gain, and a lottery ticket is a chance (albeit small) for a huge gain. You could even just agree not give gifts. But these alternatives make the potential giver look bad, so we hesitate to go this route. Sometimes we give gifts to avoid making ourselves look bad or cheap. Thus, we're still doing it for ourselves just as much as (or more than) we're doing it for others.

We can take a more complicated look at this if we include the benefit the giver gets from giving. The inefficiency of gift giving can be eliminated, but only if the value that the giver places on the act of giving is higher than the original price of the gift.

Consider an $80 gift. Suppose the giver values the giving action at $100, and the recipient values the gift at $50. Total societal benefits are $150 while costs are $80 (assuming no costs to give the gift). This is a net gain. However, it unlikely that someone values the act of giving *that* much. Further, as we stated above, people often give not for gain to themselves, but to avoid a loss on themselves (looking bad). Thus, it is more likely the giver is giving in order to incur a small loss (money spent on gift is greater than value he places on giving) instead of a big loss (looking bad or selfish for not giving).

Thus, the more realistic numbers for the $80 gift are as follows: The giver values giving at $20, and the recipient values the gift at $50. There is a $10 net loss here to society. There's actually a $60 loss incurred by the giver, but he's still giving the gift to avoid the $70 loss he would feel if his friends frowned upon him for not giving at all. Better to lose $60 than $70.

So maybe it's better not to give gifts at the holidays. Not even money. Just have the entire crew, family and friends, meet a bar or restaurant somewhere. And let everyone order what they want and have everyone pay for their own meal. People will make a cost/benefit decision for their own meal and will enjoy the extra benefit of time with family and friends.

Your Mission Trip Isn't Helping

Each year, hundreds, if not thousands, of American high school and college students go on mission trips. These young people (most likely from middle- or upper-class families) all travel to a developing country in Africa or Latin America, stay there for a week, and help locals with a task, such as erecting a small building.

This sounds great. But it's really not. It is wasteful, horribly inefficient, needlessly expensive, and may do more harm than good.

+++++++++++++++

Suppose a group of 20 college students all fly to Panama in order to build a garage for a local clinic. This costs $1,000 each (mostly travel costs) for a total expense of $20,000. If the group had just raised that much money and earmarked it for a garage through a reputable charity, a dozen garages could have been built. Remember that **purchasing power parity** doesn't hold! Your American dollars go a lot further in developing countries than they do at home. The group spent $20,000 to build a $1,500 garage.

Worse yet, when the American college kids come and build the garage, they are likely taking away work from a local builder or handyman who could have done the job. This eliminates possible revenue that could have been earned by a native resident, hurting the local economy.

Many churches and charitable organizations are taking a closer look at these short-term mission trips as they realize small benefits, high costs, and glaring inefficiencies. In fact, many churches are shifting their strategies, sending smaller groups of people (maybe even just a single family) to a location for a longer time period, where the goal is religious teaching and conversion rather than work projects. This method has costs as well, but the costs are spread out over a longer time period. The benefits for the church are arguably larger as well.

However, many humanitarian and religious groups continue to encourage and sponsor the short-term mission trips. Why do so many people keep doing this type of outreach, despite the cost and inefficiency? Consider the following quotes from mission trip testimonials. These were found just using a simple Google search for "mission trip testimonials".

- "I am humbled every day when I think back on my experience"
- "…it was one of the best things I have ever done for myself"
- "The experience made me more grateful"
- "The trip exceeded my expectations"

Read those statements again carefully. Who is mentioned in the testimonials? There is little to no mention of God from the people who participated in trips sponsored by a church. No one seems to mention the natives of the other countries.

People likely do mission trips for themselves just as much as they do it for others in need.

There is, however, a lot of 'I', 'me', and 'my' in these statements. The answer is clear: We do the mission trips for ourselves. We want to feel good about ourselves. We may even want to put a line on our resumé, or gain standing in the community by showing our charitable actions. Churches and other organizations know that people want to feel good about themselves and feel helpful and philanthropic, so they continue to offer opportunities for mission trips.

But there's a much cheaper, easier, efficient, and cost-effective way to feel good about yourselves. Find a reputable charity and just donate money. You can still brag about it to your friends.

Thank You, Gougers and Scalpers

You may be familiar with the concept of price gouging. This is generally defined as sellers raising prices during natural disasters or other extreme events. Many have very strong feelings about it, especially toward the people or businesses who price gouge. Most people see price gouging as unfair and occurring when a seller of a good unfairly jacks up prices in a greedy attempt to take advantage of helpless victims.

The word "gouging" is a poorly-defined word. If prices rise by 10%, is that alright or is it gouging? What if prices rise by 25%? Who is to say what prices are too high? Shouldn't we let buyers pay prices they are willing to pay, even if they are high? Or are high prices unfair?

But who is to say what is an "unfair" price? Why is the price being "gouged"? Shouldn't we reasonably expect prices to rise in certain situations? What happens if prices don't rise during extreme events?

+++++++++++++

Think about the economics of price gouging. In extreme situations such as a natural disaster, there is a higher demand for certain goods that most people never really needed before. This could include plywood, flashlights, batteries, gasoline, generators, non-refrigerated and ready-to-eat foods, and bottled water.

That makes sense. Those things are necessary during a natural disaster emergency. But remember your supply and demand framework from basic economics. What happens to the market for goods when there is a higher demand? The price should rise. Price gouging laws prevent sellers from raising prices, even though there is a higher demand for the goods. The law is meant to help people, but the actual result is forcing the market price to remain below the market equilibrium, and a shortage occurs. Shortages are not helpful, especially in the event of a hurricane or earthquake.

A shortage means that the buyer at the back of the line doesn't get the water or flashlights since there weren't enough stocked on the shelf to satisfy the demand at the stated price. Shortages can be exacerbated in these extreme cases because panicked people will often buy much more than they need. A person may buy ten boxes of batteries and ten cases of bottled water. The grocery store will run out of supplies soon if the first few people do that. But if the price of bottled water is legally allowed to increase to $30 a case, the people at the front won't buy ten cases – they will just buy the one case they need. And the person at the back of the line is more likely to be able to buy water for themselves.

You might not like it if bottled water is $30 per case just before the hurricane hits. But at least you'll get a chance to buy water rather than seeing an empty store shelf.

It may seem cruel to raise prices in the event of a hurricane. But doing so will help make it likely that the person in the back of the line actually gets a chance to buy goods. More importantly, it what will give sellers the incentive to bring in supplies. More supplies are what the natural disaster victims need.

One of the more famous price-gougers of recent memory is a man named John Shepperson. He was arrested for price gouging during hurricane Katrina in 2005, and his story was publicized widely at the time. He bought generators in his home state of Kentucky and tried to resell them in Mississippi for twice the price that he paid for them. According to Shepperson, people were excited to see his generators and wanted to buy from him. But police, enforcing the price gouging laws, arrested him and confiscated the remaining generators. Thus, the goods that people needed (and were willing to pay for) were forcibly removed from the market and put in police lockup rather than going to where they could be utilized most. Is this really a result that benefited society? Did price gouging laws, which are meant to help people, create a result that was in the best interest of the hurricane victims? Certainly not.

You could examine Shepperson's actions and call him immoral, greedy, or even claim that was trying to take advantage of people. But did anyone else bring generators to the hurricane victims? No. Would you have been willing to bring generators <u>without</u> raising the price to sell them, using your own gas and time?

Politically, price gouging is a strange animal. It has been defended by both liberals and conservatives. It has been condemned by both liberals and conservatives. Within economics, there tends to be similar disagreements, as it is sometimes unavoidable for people to completely ignore their personal and political leanings, despite what economics teaches us.

Perhaps because of the well-known Shepperson case, many economists wrote open letters in advance of hurricanes Harvey and Irma (both in 2017), asking officials to not prosecute price gougers. The economists invoked demand side arguments (without higher prices, people will hoard and buy more than they need) and supply side arguments (higher prices will bring in more goods, perhaps even from entrepreneurial people). Allowing prices to rise solves the problem of shortages and prevents hoarding by consumers.

> Price gougers and ticket scalpers improve economic efficiency by moving the price of goods closer to equilibrium, reducing shortages and allocating goods to people who value them most.

The same economics can be applied to ticket scalpers. Many events, from sporting events to Broadway shows, have very limited seating compared to the number of people who want to attend. Most of the time, the actual face value on the event ticket is much lower than the market equilibrium price. This, once again, results in a shortage. You've probably recalled news stories showing hundreds of people or more having repeated unsuccessful attempts trying to get tickets to shows or sporting events.

Some may just accept this as "how it is", and that it's impossible to see their favorite show or sporting event. Enter the scalper. Now, the scalper certainly has a bad reputation. He buys a large quantity of tickets and resells them at higher prices, earning a profit doing so. "How dare he!", we think. "I could have bought those tickets instead of him!" (Actually, you probably wouldn't have been able to). But economically, the scalper does something interesting – he improves economic efficiency. This is because his higher price moves the market closer to equilibrium. This helps guarantee that people who value the tickets the most get to purchase them. Harvard Economics professor Gregory Mankiw famously wrote in the New York Times that he was thankful to buy a $2,500 ticket (through StubHub) to see the musical Hamilton. He writes

> "It was only because the price was so high that I was able to buy tickets at all on such short notice. If legal restrictions or moral sanctions had forced prices to remain close to face value, it is likely that no tickets would have been available…"

If you don't care about economic efficiency and still have reservations about scalpers and other ticket resellers making a profit (and many performers do have these feelings), there is a way to put them out of business. The theater or sporting venue just needs to raise the original price of the ticket. This would reduce or eliminate markup opportunities for scalpers. Further, the higher price would help eliminate shortages (and therefore the role of the scalper) as it would reduce the size of the market to the people willing to pay more.

When legal or mainstream markets put in controls to prevent prices from rising, shortages occur. As a result, secondary (and sometimes illegal) markets are created with higher prices to allocate goods. While these secondary markets may have negative reputations, they are actually more free and more economically efficient than the "legitimate" and legal market with controlled prices.

Think Twice about College

Not everyone should go to college.

There. I said it.

+++++++++++++

If you've read this far in the book, my phrase may not seem so striking to you – but imagine if a politician running for office said that. It would likely make a good soundbite for the opposing candidate, who would claim his opponent feels that most Americans are stupid.

Young people are inundated with dogma about college from the moment they enter high school. They hear that college graduates

- Earn $30,000 more per year
- Earn $1.5 million more in their lifetime
- Are less likely to be unemployed

Institutions of higher learning spend millions of dollars trying to get more new students enrolled. When students start to look at specific colleges and universities, they'll be blasted by marketing, including advertising campaigns and materials detailing things such as

- You have more opportunities with us
- You're more likely to have a job offer after graduation with us
- You'll get paid more with a degree from us

This phenomenon isn't new. A few years (OK, a few decades) ago when I entered high school, I was told by teachers, parents, and guidance counselors, with no mincing of words, that I would turn out to be a worthless waste of space unless I went to college. All my classmates heard similar things.

The problem is that all the "good" things we hear about college (higher earnings, in particular) are simply averages. Yes, it is true that on average, college graduates earn more than high school graduates. But just because something is true for people on average, doesn't mean it is true for all individuals. Some individuals will be above the average. Others will be below. And these people that are below the average, possibly being naively fooled by simplistic data, enroll in college each year. And each year, tens of thousands of college freshmen drop out. This first-year dropout rate is a very carefully monitored statistic by colleges who are all hoping to increase retention (and therefore tuition revenues).

> We are doing our young people a great disservice by telling them that everyone must go to college to be successful.

It may sound mean, elitist, or politically incorrect to say, but many young people aren't cut out for college, for various reasons. We are doing high schoolers a great disservice by telling everyone that they must go to college. We are telling people with a high chance of failure that they need to go to college. For them, this will only lead to wasted time, wasted money, debt, and disappointment. Many people make a perfectly fine living without a four-year degree by going to a trade school, or even just working right out of high school. The jobs they get may be different from a college graduate, but that is OK. We need a variety of people with a variety of skills to create a variety of goods and services. And if people enjoy their jobs, we shouldn't act elitist and look down upon them for lack of a college degree. In fact, maybe we should admire them for getting a job they enjoy without incurring $40,000 of tuition debt.

To all the people who matriculate and remain in college, they get herded into some pretty crowded classrooms. Perhaps eventually, this large group of students will graduate. But what happens when the supply of college graduates increases? Generally, you'll recall from your economics class that when the supply of something increases, its price goes down. In other words, if everyone has a college degree, the degree won't mean anything special anymore and will lose value. People will have to soon race further to the top and get a Master's degree or MBA to distinguish themselves. But so far, the demand for college graduates has increased in line with supply, keeping the degree valuable. Firms seem to want to hire college graduates, which has kept wages of college graduates higher. But one must wonder if the demand increase can keep up with the supply increase for much longer. If supply outpaces demand, the value of the degree will fall.

Unfortunately, even many of these people that go on to graduate college will remain disappointed. This can happen for two reasons. First, the big college graduate salary might never come. Second, college is very expensive and can create crushing debt (just in case you were unaware of this).

Many people graduate college, and shockingly end up in a job that is unrelated to their chosen field of study. There are a lot of history majors who don't become historians or curators. There are A LOT of psychology majors. They certainly do not all become psychologists, psychiatrists, or academics in their field. Many of these people end up taking office jobs, sales jobs, construction work, or whatever else is available. Thus, the 4 years of tuition (and 4 years of time, not earning money!) that was spent in college may not result in larger pay. Many of those jobs could have been done without the degree.

Second, college is expensive. You have to pay for it. Even if your future job doesn't pay well, you still owe State U those tuition dollars.

Unsurprisingly, we have arrived at the commonly-asked question: why is college so expensive? There are two reasons for this: administrative and facility bloat, as well as easy money being loaned to students.

Colleges have become extremely top-heavy with middle- and upper-level administrators. Presidents, deans, provosts, chancellors, heads, directors (as well as 'vice's and 'assistant's to those titles) are all hired, paid well, and likely do little to no teaching. These people are hired for the increasingly bureaucratic operations of higher education. Ask any employee at an institute of higher learning, and they'll tell you that there has to be a "task force" or "committee" for every single little thing. Someone has to run and oversee these task forces. And someone has to manage the overseers.

Further, colleges and universities are all guilty of wasteful facility spending and creating Potemkin Villages. There are expensive, new, and flashy areas on campus that you will certainly be escorted to on a campus visit. There may be state-of-the-art research labs and a brand new glass blowing studio, all expensive to build. But in reality, very few undergraduate students will ever get to spend meaningful time in these places and will instead be relegated to regular classrooms. These regular classrooms are conveniently hidden from your tour path and are often sadly in need of repairs and upgrades.

The second reason why college is so expensive is counterintuitive. With high tuition prices, you might be thankful that there are so many student loans available, many of them even backed by the federal government. But we have an example of reverse causality here. The loans don't exist because college is expensive. College is expensive because of the loans! Easily available student loans are not the solution to the college cost problem – they are very much a part of the cause.

How is this the case? Think about it like this – if all students are easily able to get $60,000 in student loans, colleges can effectively treat students like they are $60,000 richer and will raise tuition accordingly. As another example, suppose the President loves to golf, and therefore offered everyone a $3,000 government-backed loan that could only be used toward the purchase of a new golf cart, and these loans had 0% interest for four years.

> It might seem a little counterintuitive at first, but easy-to-acquire student loans are not the solution to high college tuition. Rather, they are a big part of the problem and contribute to rising tuition costs.

Does anyone think that golf cart sellers *wouldn't* raise their prices? Golf cart sellers could easily and quietly raise the price of a cart by $600 since everyone now had more money specifically to buy carts. When easy money is available, prices rise. The upper administration of the institutes of higher learning are not dumb. When colleges know that easy money is available, they will be able to raise tuition each year without much pushback from students and parents.

The solution to this problem is to simply make loans harder to get. Don't have loans backed or subsidized by the federal government. It sounds a bit counterintuitive to say that taking away potential money from students will make college more affordable – but easy student loan money has allowed colleges to be unfettered with their tuition increases. If fewer students are able to get loans, or if fewer students want to get loans, colleges will be forced to be more price competitive, and tuition rates will fall (or at least increase at much slower rates).

Take all of this into consideration when making the college decision, either for yourself or for your kids someday. Remember that:

- Just because a statistic is true on average, it doesn't mean it is true for all individuals.
- College is expensive. Not only is tuition expensive, but you'll also be giving up four or five years of earning money since you'll be a student rather than an employee.
- Having a college diploma won't automatically result in a high-paying job.

Don't listen to the hype of "everyone should go to college". Make your own decision based on your own likelihood of succeeding.

Illegal Immigration is Probably OK

With the election of President Trump in 2016 came chants of "build that wall". Specifically, a wall on the border of the United States and Mexico with the goal of keeping out illegal immigrants. The fight against illegal immigration usually comes from the conservative side of the aisle, and includes talking points such as:

- Illegal immigrants are free-riders who don't pay taxes, who leech on our society
- Illegal immigrants take jobs from Americans and depress wages
- Illegal immigrants are criminals

We can examine each of these points.

+++++++++++++

While illegal immigrants may not pay income taxes if they are paid under the table, they still buy goods in the United States and pay sales tax. The National Academies found that while illegal immigrants may have negative effects for state and local taxes, federal tax effects may net to be positive. Further, their report states that children of immigrants are among the highest economic and fiscal contributors, even paying more in taxes than the native-born population. Over time, this may result in illegal immigrants being net taxpayers, meaning they pay more in taxes than they would receive in tax-funded benefits.

With regards to jobs, these immigrants provide labor for many sectors that are labor-intensive, including construction and certain agricultural sectors. These jobs can be difficult, dangerous, unpleasant, uncomfortable, require working outdoors all day in the heat, and involve a lot of lifting. In other words, they are the types of jobs that skilled or educated people would want to avoid. Thus, it is fallacious to assume that illegal immigrants are taking jobs from

Americans or pushing down the wages of hard-working Americans. These are the jobs that legal residents or American citizens would not perform, at least at the wages being offered by the employers.

Immigrants really do take the jobs that Americans don't want. Thus, the argument that immigrants depress American wages doesn't have a lot of merit, with the possible exception of extremely low-skilled American workers, such as high school dropouts.

For example, take the well-documented experiment done by Alabama tomato farmer Jerry Spencer in 2011. After tough laws against illegal immigrants were passed in the state, he tried to get US citizens to work for him, even giving them free transportation. Of the 50 people he recruited for the work, only a few worked for more than three days. Only one person lasted in the job for two weeks. Undocumented labor crackdowns will continue to hurt agricultural productivity as farmers will be unable to find workers to help in the fields. In another story from 2011, tomato farmer Brian Cash tells how he used to have a workforce of 65 Hispanics to pick tomatoes. Now he has none, and the result is hundreds of thousands of dollars of unpicked and rotting fruit each year. Does wasted and rotting food really help the economy? Is this in anyone's best interest?

Now, the undocumented workers that take these jobs are often paid illegally in cash. This of course eliminates paperwork and evidence of using illegal labor. But it also means the income is not taxed. Since the labor is not taxed and the workers may not have other job opportunities, the pay is often lower. This may seem exploitative. First of all, it is illegal to pay workers cash under the table – this is a black market. But remember that black markets tend to develop when market participants feel there are problems, inefficiencies, or difficulties with legal markets. If a farmer or construction firm can't find people to work for the lower pay, or can't afford to pay legal workers the high wages they demand, they find people who can work and receive the lower cash payments illegally. While this is illegal, it is not exploitative. The farmers and construction managers need workers, and the workers need jobs. The parties agree on payment and work, and mutually beneficial trade is done. If the workers really felt exploited or taken advantage of, they would not accept the work.

The only way to fill these jobs with legal labor would be to pay the workers a lot more money. In 2017, the LA Times reported that farmworkers in California earn well above the minimum wage, and farmers are giving retirement plans, health insurance, and housing to workers. But despite this, 90% of farm workers in the state are foreign-born. Maybe Americans just aren't willing to do the tomato picking job unless they get paid $300 a day. But higher wages will inevitably lead to higher food prices. Thus, we could try to pat ourselves on the back by being tough on immigration and using American workers, but we would be discouraged when we see that produce prices have doubled at the grocery store.

It is frustrating to see liberals almost never using these above talking points as arguments when discussing what to do about illegal immigration. These are powerful economic arguments about immigrants paying taxes, providing work, producing goods, and keeping food prices low. Immigrants are extremely beneficial to agriculture and construction industries. But sadly, these arguments go unspoken. Unfortunately, liberals often just use arguments such as "people aren't illegal" and "your ancestors emigrated" and "deportation is racist". These are just emotion-based arguments and have much less persuasive power.

A possible solution is to have temporary guest worker programs, where immigrants come to the United States with seasonal jobs waiting for them. The workers can come, work, get paid, and then return to their families. This would create a win-win situation for farmers and workers.

What to do about illegal immigration? Well, if an undocumented person is arrested or put into custody for any of various reasons, we can deport them to their home country. But the costs of spending resources just for the sake of looking for illegal immigrants (in order to deport them) outweighs the benefits.

A guest worker program would allow our country to reap the benefits of immigrants (a supply of labor willing to do jobs that Americans don't want). It would further allow better tracking of immigrants to assuage concerns of undocumented immigrants remaining in the country illegally or getting involved in other illegal activities.

What about the crime data? Do illegal immigrants commit more crimes? According to factcheck.org, there are studies which say yes, and others that say no. We don't have enough nationwide statistics on crimes committed by undocumented immigrants. Many smaller localized studies have come to conclusions that illegal immigrants commit less crime and are less likely to be incarcerated than American citizens. If this is true, one possible reason is that the cost of getting arrested is higher as they would ultimately be deported.

One final thing to remember: About half of the illegal immigrants in the United States aren't people who climbed over a wall or crawled through a tunnel to get here. They are people who came here legally on student or work visas, but then overstayed that visa. These types of immigrants are likely to be higher-skilled than those who cross the border illegally, so deportation efforts against this demographic are likely to have higher costs and much lower benefits. Thus, they are likely not going to be as pressing of a matter.

Let's Pay College Athletes

If you watch ESPN or other networks that contain sports news and commentary, you've probably heard dozens of talking heads say negative things about the NCAA.

- Their punishments are too harsh
- Their punishments aren't harsh enough
- Their punishments are inconsistent
- Their rules are too strict
- Their rules aren't strict enough
- The athletes are being exploited

Many of these end up being opinions based on which school is facing NCAA sanctions at the time. They always go easy on the other schools, and they went way overboard on my school.

The last argument has become more prevalent lately. The athletes of the NCAA are being exploited. Very specifically, it seems unfair to many that these athletes are not getting paid (and are not allowed to get paid) while universities and coaches are earning millions from the work and effort of the athletes.

+++++++++++++

How has this system evolved to where it is today? One could debate about amateur versus professional sports and make statements that college kids are amateurs, so they therefore should not be paid. Others argue that college athletes are paid through scholarships.

First, the professional versus amateur argument doesn't hold water when it comes to paying a salary to players. Professional and amateur are just different titles. There are also skill differences, but that alone should not justify a salary of zero for college athletes. Long ago, Olympic athletes were not allowed to be paid nor were they allowed to be compensated for endorsement deals. The result of this was lower-quality athletes. The better athletes knew there was a lot of money to be made with endorsements, so they would forego the Olympics. It wasn't until 1986 that the rules were changed to allow professional athletes to complete in the Olympics.

What about the scholarship argument? Many athletes get scholarships. But many don't. Even those that do, the amount of the scholarship is very small compared to the amount of time, work, and effort provided by the athlete.

The anticompetitiveness of the NCAA has allowed it to take advantage of collegiate athletes and push wages down to zero.

We further need to admit the concept of "student athlete" (a favorite phrase by the NCAA) is often a farce. Most elite players in the big sports (football, men's basketball) are not in college for an education. They are there to play sports. Note that there is nothing wrong with this! The player is just hoping to become a professional someday, and going through the college sports system of the NCAA is the only method to achieve that goal. The University knows these students aren't there for an education, and will help them limp through classes with tutors, study groups, preferred class schedules, preferred courses, and in extreme cases, fake classes (see the University of North Carolina incident where the school was inexplicably spared NCAA sanctions for offering fake classes for athletes).

The economics of this situation involves a strange word used almost exclusively in labor markets. That word is *monopsony* – a situation where there is just one buyer of a good. Note that this is different from *monopoly*, where there is just one seller of a good. In a monopoly, you expect prices to be high since buyers have no choice. But in a monopsony, prices are low because there is only one buyer – therefore, sellers must accept the low price the only buyer is willing to pay. In the market for college amateur athletes, there is only one buyer. And that one buyer, the NCAA, pushed the price of college athlete labor down to zero. Collegiate athletes have to accept this low price since there is no other place for them to play and compete. In most markets, this extreme level of non-competitiveness would lead to antitrust lawsuits. It is also why some University athletes are leading charges to unionize and demand better conditions and pay.

The anticompetitiveness of the NCAA has also allowed it to get away with a lot of bizarre rules historically. It's micromanaging gone awry, in which any sort of perceived benefit given to an athlete can result in sanctions. Some infamous examples:

- In 2013, some University of Oklahoma football players had to pay $3.83 to charity to restore their eligibility because they ate too much pasta at a graduation banquet.
- In 2000, Nebraska quarterback Eric Crouch had to donate $22.77 to charity because of a ham sandwich and plane ride that were considered impermissible benefits.
- Until 2013, the NCAA had a bagel rule, in which schools could give athletes bagels, but cream cheese and peanut butter were considered impermissible benefits.

The NCAA finally lifted their strange food portion rules in 2015. But the rules about impermissible phone calls and car rides remain.

When there is a price ceiling of zero on college athlete wages, black markets will develop. The extent of these underground markets came to light in early 2018 with a bombshell report providing details in which more than 20 Division I programs had provided five- and six-figure payments to athletes and their families. There are likely more schools that do this but have continued to get away with it.

This seems shady, but only because the NCAA made it illegal. In almost all other markets, workers are compensated for their time, effort, and the revenue they generate for the firm. But despite the fact that these athletes generate millions of dollars for universities, the NCAA insists on not allowing them to be paid legally – so they get paid illegally. This is a market at work. It is a black market, but it is a free market with negotiations and beneficial trades. It seems as if

NCAA elite athletes will get paid no matter what – so why not make a system that allows above-ground payments?

Another example of a monopsonistic labor market in athletics is the WNBA. At the beginning of the WNBA, all teams were owned by the WNBA (as opposed to the NBA, where all teams had different and competing owners). The result of this single ownership of all teams led to another anticompetitive monopsony, where the WNBA was the only buyer of labor for professional women's basketball. The result was absurdly low pay. On average, an entire WNBA team's combined salary was less than the salary of a single NBA player. Yes, there could be demand reasons for this as well (not as many people were interested in viewing WNBA games or buying tickets), but the main driver of that low pay was the fact that there was no competition to bid up salaries on the best players. The WNBA teams are now finally owned by separate and competing owners, but the pay for players remains low. This is in part because the previous pay set a low standard (a point of reference, if you will), and pay has not adjusted much from that original level.

The NCAA could be a sub-professional league with athletes getting paid. If we still desire some sort of regulation, there can be salary caps, just like the professional leagues. Or perhaps other structures could be used, such as each university having five basketball players that are paid $80,000, five that are paid $40,000, while the rest of the roster receives $20,000. There are a number of possible solutions that could be implemented, or at least tried on a pilot program. But one thing is certain – the current system isn't working. The anticompetitiveness of the NCAA forces athletes to get zero pay, so universities and athletes have the incentive to create and participate in black markets. Universities that actually play by the rules are hurt with lower quality athletes since the higher quality athletes are likely accepting impermissible benefits from "cheating" schools. The current system punishes those who play by the rules, and benefits those who cheat (as long as they don't get caught). But the punishments of getting caught just serve as an incentive to push the market even further underground, hiding evidence of its existence.

Take More Risks and Be More Careful

In an introductory economics course, you'll learn that decision making should be done using cost-benefit analysis. A decision will improve a person's well-being if the marginal benefits are greater than the marginal costs.

+++++++++++++

This is deceptively easy. The problem with real life is that possible costs and benefits are often not known with certainty ahead of time. Or worse, we might not even know the probability of gaining benefits or incurring costs. For example, there are many types of gambles one could take in life, and we may even quickly make the decision, using roughshod estimation of success and failure probabilities.

> By focusing too much on possible losses rather than possible gains, we tend to play it safe more often.

This can be done with anything from passing a car on a highway, to not setting your alarm before bed, or even copying a friend's homework. We make decisions every day, and sometimes we come out ahead. On days where we come out not so good, it doesn't mean that we are dumb. It means we may have miscalculated some probabilities. It could also mean that we were lazy and wanted to take a shortcut – and we thought that taking shortcuts had a higher probability of success than it really did.

Economists have discovered that by and large, people tend to be risk averse. This means we prefer to avoid taking risks. We would rather take a certain relatively low benefit, even if another option involves the probability of earning a higher benefit. For example, I could offer you a certain $10, or offer you a coin-flip game where heads gives you $20 and tails gives you nothing. The coin flip game has the higher maximum possible payout, but the average payout of both the game and the certain money is the same at $10. However, most people will opt for the certain $10. People with even higher levels of risk aversion may even take a certain $5 instead of playing the same $20 coin flip game. Perhaps people just like to have something certain that they can "bank".

People also tend to have loss aversion. This means that losing $20 feels worse than gaining $20 feels good. In other words, we hate losing more than we like winning.

I want you to take more risks. But only if you absorb all the costs and consequences of that risk.

Perhaps this is a feeling you can relate to. But the problem is that risk aversion and loss aversion can cause us to avoid taking risks, even when it might be in our best interest to do so. This results in us foregoing decisions that would make us better off!

So go out and try to start that business. Take some money (not your mortgage payment!) and invest in some high-risk, high-return investments.

Not all risks involve money. Risk could also be associated with asking that special person on a date, moving to a new city without a perfect job lined up yet, or even calling in sick to work when you're completely healthy so you can go to the ballgame. Go ahead – take the risks. The outcome is more likely to be favorable than you might think.

Now if you read the title of this section, you'll see something about taking risks *and* being more careful. How can you do both of those things?

First, notice the examples of risks mentioned above. If you happen to fail at that new job, get turned down by your dream date, or get seen by the boss at the ballgame, all the costs are borne by you. Nobody else is harmed if your gamble doesn't pay off.

We tend to take too few risks when we ourselves bear the full costs and consequences of failure. But people take more risks when some or all of the costs associated with the risk are paid by *others*. That makes perfect economic sense from a basic cost/benefit analysis. If my costs of the activity decrease, I'll be more likely to do the activity. The problem is that the costs don't go away completely – they are just shouldered by other people. But since we don't often think about the costs and benefits of other people, we ignore these outside costs and will do more of the risky behavior.

This is the definition of **moral hazard**. Moral hazard occurs when people take advantage of situations in which costs of an activity can be passed on to others. If my benefits are the same but other people are paying part of the costs, I'll be more likely to engage in the activity compared to a scenario where I had to pay all costs myself.

Moral hazard is usually discussed in health care economics, in which people tend to overuse health care as the result of having insurance. When insurance pays, people may overuse health care since they still get the benefits with much lower marginal costs.

But with general risk taking, moral hazard means that people may not be as careful when others subsidize the risk.

Here are some examples:

- A student whose parents are paying for his college tuition is more likely to party every weekend than someone who is working a fulltime job to put themselves through college.
- A student whose parents pay for his car and insurance is more likely to drive recklessly compared to a student who pays for his own vehicle and insurance.
- People remain unemployed longer if they live in a country or state with more generous unemployment benefits.

Is moral hazard a problem? Certainly in health care it is, as it can drive up insurance prices for everyone. It is also problematic if unemployment insurance results in longer bouts of employment for the typical workers. But what about other situations? Why should we care if a trust fund kid wrecks his new car or parties her way through college?

The policy concern about moral hazard arises when the costs of the risk ultimately fall on the public. For example, if you build your home in a region that is prone to flooding or hurricanes, you'll have to pay higher insurance rates to cover this added risk. However, you do not pay the full price of this risk, as much of it is subsidized by the government. In other words, the taxpayers are paying for your risks.

Government subsidized flood insurance programs incentivize people to build homes in areas that are at risk of flooding. When the floods come, the bill is paid by the taxpayers rather than the homeowners.

The National Flood Insurance Program (NFIP) is the largest example of this. The program currently insures about 5 million homes, but is over $25 billion in debt, owing money to the U.S. Treasury. Since people don't have to the pay the "fair price" of insurance that reflects the actual risk of flooding and hurricanes, more people live in flood-prone areas and don't take necessary flood prevention precautions. Many of these homes are in Texas and Florida, owned by the very wealthy (think beachfront properties), and have repeated insurance claims on them.

Other criticisms of the NFIP claim that it hurts low-income people as well. Due to NFIP rules about occupancy and loss coverage, many owners rent out these properties rather than live there themselves. This rent may be offered at a discount to attract renters, and the discount may attract lower income or elderly people, who are less likely able to recover from a flood when belongings are destroyed.

When subsidized programs reduce the risk of owning and building in flood zones, demand increases. When flooding or hurricanes happen, this will increase the cost of damages, but the subsidies have still kept private costs low, and climate change may exacerbate this issue in the future. We see moral hazard in action here. A property owner is able to pass the costs and risks of flooding to others, encouraging more building in flood prone areas. Other taxpayers are on the hook, even if they choose to avoid risk and not build in flood zones.

Consider another example of moral hazard related to hurricanes. In anticipation of a major storm, cities and states often issue mandatory evacuation orders. And every year, hundreds of people ignore these orders. These people then need to be rescued, which risks the lives of police officers, the National Guard, first responders, or even just good Samaritans trying to help.

Why do so many people ignore the evacuation order? For one, evacuation can be costly with time and effort. It may take a lot of effort to get supplies, board up, and pack up. It may take a lot of time to evacuate on crowded roads and highways. Further, people know that there is relatively high probability of getting rescued if things get really bad and you can call for help. People also know there is a relatively low probability that they'll have to pay for their rescue.

The problem is that these rescues are not free. It costs money to search with boats and helicopters, and the rescues can even be dangerous for the rescuers. But since the costs of the rescue are not paid by the person needing the rescuing, more people are likely to ignore the evacuation order to avoid the costs of leaving.

It may sound heartless to make hurricane victims pay for their own rescue, but doing so would increase compliance with evacuation orders, and would reduce the costs and risks associated with performing rescues in dangerous areas after the storm. We are not making them pay for the storm, we are making them pay for the fact that they willingly ignored the safety order and put others' lives at risk to save them. Think of it as a recklessness tax.

There are many other cases where people need to be rescued: a climber or skier stuck on a mountain, a hiker lost in the forest, a swimmer struggling in a lake or ocean. When outdoorsmen or extreme athletes get into trouble in remote areas and require rescue, should they foot the bill?

Taxpayers will be benefitted if people have to pay for their own rescues. Such legislation will reduce the amount of recklessness that results in someone needing rescued.

A quick Google search will review that there is a lively debate about this topic. Some people think of rescuing as a public service, but others note cases of woefully underprepared and inexperienced people venturing out far beyond their ability, resulting in rescues costing tens of thousands of dollars. One point of agreement is that there is a difference between an accident and willful recklessness. The fire department doesn't send you a bill if your house catches on fire, but your insurance company may certainly inspect the cause of the fire before paying a claim. We could be more sympathetic to an accident that could happen to anyone (slipping, falling, getting injured). But if someone ventures into the forest on a hike with no food, no water, no flashlight, all while wearing flip flops, perhaps they could be billed for rescuing them from their own negligence. New Hampshire, for example, has a law making anyone who acts "negligently in requiring a search and rescue response" liable for their own rescue.

The New Hampshire law is aimed to reduce the moral hazard of willful negligence. Once again, this boils down to the incentives of individuals. When we make people pay for their own risks, they'll be more careful. We will not have to put rescuers in as much danger. And the taxpaying public will be happier.

Let Rich White People Kill Elephants and Lions

In 2015, dentist Walter Palmer from Bloomington, Minnesota shot a lion on a game hunt in Africa. This sort of thing had happened before, but this time, everyone went nuts.

This lion had a *name*! It was Cecil the Lion. He was known to visitors of the Hwange National Park in Zimbabwe and was being tracked by a research team as part of a long-term study.

The situation became a sensationalized national news story.

This story might make you sick, sad, or uncomfortable. But what if the best way to save big game is to allow hunting?

++++++++++++++

It's important to note that these lions were not endangered at the time. They are listed as endangered now, but only because the U.S. Fish and Wildlife Service (which had already been questionably acting far outside of its jurisdiction when it tried to conduct investigations and searches in Africa) put certain species of lions on the endangered list 5 months after the Cecil killing. This was done not because of population declines in those 5 months, but rather as a political response to placate the outraged public and to make lions harder to hunt.

Palmer also had a legal permit and had legally purchased a guide hunt. The lion was killed in an area without a quota for kills. There were no crimes ever charged against Palmer in Zimbabwe or the United States, and all charges that were originally brought against his hunting guide were thrown out.

Despite the facts that

- the hunt was legal
- lions were not endangered
- likely less than a few dozen people in the entire United States had even heard of this lion before the hunt
- the death of the lion had absolutely zero effect on our lives here

the situation quickly became the outrage du jour. People protested at Palmer's place of work, and he was forced to close his practice. Thus, all his staff, assistants, and hygienists lost their jobs, and his patients lost their dentist. Most of the angry people in their knee-jerk outrage, wanting to punish this evil dentist, caused harm far beyond him. Real people, who had nothing to do with hunt, lost their livelihoods – all because of protestors' feelings for an animal they'd never heard of the week before. Maybe people were too focused on the lion and not focused enough on the human collateral damage caused by the horde of moral outrage.

As absurd as the protests against Palmer were, I'll save my rant against the angry mob for another day. Rather, I'll write here to stick up for Palmer and his hunting guide. Economists and conservationists have seen empirical evidence that shows legal hunting actually increases the population of the big game animals.

Wait… how could that possibly make sense? The best way to save species (preventing extinction and encouraging a large enough breeding population) is to allow hunting? That sounds ludicrous.

Actually, it's not. It's all about property rights and ownership. And when people have ownership over something, they are more likely to take care of it.

Consider elephants. Many countries (including Botswana and Kenya) have simply outlawed the hunting and killing of elephants. But this has not worked. It has not stopped poachers and elephant numbers continue to decline. Simply making poaching illegal has not been a strong enough incentive for police in those countries to put in the time and effort to search vast areas and stop poaching. The act of making hunting unlawful also does not provide any funding to support anti-poaching efforts.

But in other countries (South Africa, Zimbabwe, Namibia, and Zambia) the local people have a form of ownership and property rights over the elephants. They sell hunting licenses, often to the titular rich white people. These hunting permits can sell for tens of thousands of dollars and include a guided hunt from locals. Thus, the local people have a very strong financial incentive to take care of the elephant population and stop illegal poaching. In these countries where hunting is legal and expensive licenses are sold, elephant populations have been steadily increasing. The guides also strategically target which elephants to hunt, such as an aging male rather than a breeding-age female, to further keep populations high and growing. Many of these guides and others involved in anti-poaching efforts are even former poachers themselves. Now they have a reason to protect the population rather than just killing everything they can for ivory.

> Banning trophy hunting may seem like a good way to save big game populations.
> But this has not worked.

Even the Fish and Wildlife Service seems to be in favor of allowing legal elephant hunting. In a news release, it stated that "legal, well-managed hunting programs" provide money which will aid conservation efforts. The International Union for Conservation of Nature supports this as well. Kenya outlawed elephant hunting in 1973, but is currently considering allowing trophy hunting after seeing positive results in Namibia and South Africa.

A possible problem is that much of the (American) public doesn't support it. Even though many Americans may have no knowledge of hunting, conservation, or have any idea of how the legal hunting permits operate, people will still certainly be willing to share their opinion about how any hunting of big game should be illegal. People are outraged that it's legal, as evidenced by the protests against Walter Palmer. But in economics, we look at data rather than opinions. The data shows that where hunting is legal, populations are increasing. Hunting generates money and gives locals the incentive to take care of the animals and stop poachers.

But do we really have to do the hunting and killing? Is there ANY other way? If there is, we haven't found it yet. Other ideas, such as fundraisers, donations, charities, and awareness campaigns may raise some money. Tougher laws and penalties may discourage some poachers. But ultimately, none of these methods make the big game animals more valuable. It's property rights over the animals and the hunting licenses that make the big game valuable, thus providing the locals the incentive to take care of the populations and stop poachers.

I would probably agree that killing elephants and other big game sounds disgusting. But it's working, and it's resulted in increasing populations. I certainly don't want to discourage the reader from looking for alternatives, though. Go find something else that raises as much money for anti-poaching efforts and incentivizes locals to take care of the species. I'm sure the elephants are all ears.

Should we go "Full Socialist" to get Equality?

Most casual observers would note that politics has become more partisan in recent years. This has perhaps been a result of populist candidates, with politicians and voters becoming more extreme in their views. Republicans have become more conservative, even aiming to eliminate protections for certain groups and hoping to overturn Roe vs. Wade. Democrats have become more like socialists, especially in their economic ideas.

To the economically uninitiated, socialism seems good. Doesn't it sound nice for everyone to be equal and to be taken care of by the government? As I said, it sounds good to some. But it ends up working for none.

+++++++++++++

Socialism has a goal of making everyone equal. An egalitarian society. But socialism doesn't lift everyone up to the top. Rather, it brings everyone down to the bottom. It works by taking from the rich (forcefully) and giving to the poor. Once again, this might sound good to some. But in economics, we learn all about incentives from day one. If any excess wealth will be taken away, the incentives to work hard and accumulate wealth has been effectively destroyed. And when people quit working hard, economic growth, technological progress, and investing in the future will cease.

There are a lot of misperceptions about the rich. The word 'rich' even tends to have a negative connotation. Is this just the result of our jealousy?

If rising above others in income and wealth results in it being taken away from you, why bother to work hard? If the government goal is to make everyone equal, why bother to work at all? It's going to be much easier to free-ride and get equal endings without the work.

Here are some fallacies about inequality:

- Rich people just inherited their money
- You can only get rich by keeping others poor
- Money is zero-sum. Your gain must be someone else's loss
- Rich people cheated or somehow otherwise took advantage of others to get their fortunes

These fallacies are extremely and stubbornly pervasive. Perhaps it is the result of parents telling it to their kids, or teachers telling it to students. But to be honest, a lot of these fallacies are rooted in jealously. Someone has something more than I do, therefore it isn't right and they must have cheated. I am going to see their gains as ill-gotten. I am going to despise them because of their wealth.

Here are some facts:

- Most billionaires are self-made
- Capitalism has been shown historically time and time again as the best economic system to increase the well-being of <u>all</u> people, rich and poor
- Trade improves the well-being of both buyers and sellers

Before we go further, remember the difference between income and wealth. Income is a flow, wealth is a stock. Income can be thought of how much money you're bringing in per year, and wealth can be thought of as your current total sum of everything you own. Take an extreme form of socialism, in which all <u>wealth</u> is pooled, and distributed evenly among all people in the country. Everyone is now equal. But even if this could somehow be done, it wouldn't last long. Different people have different jobs, and those jobs will provide different income. Thus, the people with higher incomes will add to their wealth quickly and surpass those with lower or no incomes.

Thus, we haven't reached our equality goal. Something more extreme is required.

A more extreme step to guarantee equality would be to try to redistribute wealth *and* to make sure everyone has the same income. Doctors, janitors, teachers, and even the unemployed will now have the same income each year and start with the same wealth. (This already is sounding bad. Incentives to get an education and work hard have already been destroyed in this scenario). But even this won't guarantee equality for more than a generation. Some will have had to spend more since they had more children to support. Some would have just blown through their money for various other reasons. Some people will have saved more money than others. Thus, by the time the next generation starts, some kids may have inherited money from their parents. And that's not fair! Let's add on a 100% inheritance tax to fix this problem!

Thus, you can see how unrealistic absolute equality is. It destroys incentives to work hard, would require huge amounts of oversight and regulation to redistribute wealth and fix pay, and would likely lead to economic collapse quickly. Socialists would say they aren't arguing for absolute equality or equal incomes in all jobs, but many have argued in favor of a 100% inheritance tax. The logic is that some get an unfair start in life, and this amplifies inequality, so we should make everyone start on equal footing. (Once again, you see that this is an example of making people equal by taking down the rich rather than bringing up the poor. The poor neighbor isn't any better because a wealthy neighbor is disallowed from leaving money to his kid, but socialists somehow disagree). This 100% inheritance tax would slow down economic growth greatly.

Consider Nobel Prize winning economist Milton Friedman. When asked about a 100% inheritance tax by a student at a public question and answer forum, he gave this response:

> "The only way in which you can redistribute, effectively, the wealth, is by destroying the incentives to have wealth...
> What is the effect of a 100% inheritance tax? It is to

encourage people to dissipate their wealth in high living. The harm in that is, where do you get the factories? Where do you get the machines? Where do you get the capital investments? Where do you get the incentive to improve technology? If what you're doing is to establish a society, in which the incentive is for people – who if by accident accumulate some wealth – to waste it in frivolous entertainment… It would destroy a continuing society."

The Friedman quote illustrates that problem with a 100% inheritance tax more eloquently than I ever could. Simply put, it would destroy any incentive to save or invest. It would eliminate growth and perhaps society itself.

Finally, even if there was a 100% inheritance tax with the hopes of giving everyone an "equal start", it is worth to remember something important – Equal opportunity doesn't not mean equal results. Even if you force equal opportunity, you can't force equal results. No matter what we try to manipulate or social engineer, some people will be successful, and some people won't. Some people are smarter, taller, faster, more charismatic, better public speakers, or have more skills. Some people might just work harder or for more hours. Some people are better at saving money than others. Some people will end up ahead, and some people will end up behind.

Equal opportunity and equal results are two very different things. Equal opportunity is given to all. We can all succeed in this country. But socialists ultimately want to force equal results, which eliminates incentives to put in work and effort.

We must be careful with our laws, policies, and the people we elect to make and enforce these laws. We do not want to punish success and destroy the incentives to work hard all in the name of attempted equality. We certainly also do not want to incentivize apathetic torpor with overly generous government programs and handouts. Doing so would cripple any economic growth we could hope to achieve.

Any economic system – capitalism, communism, or socialism – must answer questions about scarcity. This includes questions about production, resource allocation, and what determines which people end up with goods and services. Do we want markets (supply and demand) to determine what is made and who gets the goods, or do we want government to play a larger role (or the only role) in this allocation?

Capitalism certainly doesn't result in absolute equality. But perhaps that's the point. We want to incentivize and reward productivity. If you're still concerned about the poor, all we need to do is make some historical

Socialism just redistributes the pie, helping some while harming others.

Capitalism makes the pie bigger, helping everyone.

comparisons. We've seen that throughout history, capitalism is the economic system which has repeatedly shown that it is the best economic system to improve the lives of all people, rich and poor. Capitalism results in the pie getting bigger where everyone can get more, and everyone can benefit. Socialism just results in the same size of pie getting cut in a different way, where some people are helped and some people are hurt, but the overall economy stagnates.

Despite this, capitalism usually gets results that are more equal than communist or socialist countries. And the drivers of inequality are different. In communist countries, inequality exists as a result of the poor being very poor. This is often due to allocation issues in which corrupt officials steal from the people. In capitalist countries, inequality exists because the rich are very rich. This isn't because the rich stole from the poor – it is because they created and profited from something deemed valuable by markets. It is clear that one of these outcomes seems much more problematic than the other.

Due to the forceful nature of redistribution and need for larger government, socialism and communism are also much more likely to be paired with oppressive governments that erode or eliminate personal freedoms. This is a natural consequence of the systems. When the government needs more power in determining outcomes, it takes away the power of people to control outcomes.

Ask yourselves this: Why are people always fleeing from communist countries? It's because they are trying to escape oppressive governments and crushing poverty. At any time in history, have there ever been cases of people trying to get out of a capitalist country, so they could flee TO a communist country? No.

Legalize It

So far, I've voiced support to allow hunting of big game and payments to college athletes. But we don't have to stop there.

In the United States, there are many goods and activities that are currently illegal (or that are not legal but effectively decriminalized) which could be traded in legal markets with great benefits.

Perhaps you are thinking of marijuana, but we can take it further and discuss legalizing other drugs and prostitution as well.

Our government has the power to dictate that is illegal to consume, trade, or own certain goods and services. A common justification is that they're trying to protect the citizens. But we have already seen that when behavior is criminalized, this often does not stop the action but rather leads to the creation of black markets. And these black markets, due to their hidden and unregulated nature, are often more dangerous for participants compared to if the activity had been legal.

+++++++++++++

There has recently certainly been a push to legalize marijuana in the United States. I am/was extremely happy to see that the arguments for this are very closely related to economics. A big pro-legalization argument is related to money and public resources. Instead of spending police resources and millions of dollars to incarcerate non-violent offenders, we could turn marijuana into a revenue *creating* good, with high taxes on legal goods (similar to cigarettes). Other economic arguments in favor of legalization invoke the rights and freedoms of individuals and states to make their own decisions rather than having a federal government decide what is best for everyone. People want to have decentralized decision making by many people rather than centralized planning and laws from the top.

I likely don't have to spend much time talking about the legalization of marijuana as it is already gaining broader support. But what about other drugs? What about prostitution?

Many activities are banned with the reasoning that they could harm ourselves or others. However, a common irony is that banning a behavior because it is unsafe may make the activity even more dangerous to the participants involved.

As much as I've spoken against government involvement and intervention in this text, our government certainly does *some* good. The Department of Justice enforces antitrust laws that can hopefully improve market efficiency, promote competition, and discourage rent-seeking monopolistic attempts in non-competitive industries. The FDA and CPSC can hopefully improve the safety of food and other consumables. The FAA, TSA, and NTSB can oversee and investigate travel safety issues. These organizations are not immune to criticism, and there is certainly debate on how much (or little) they should do. But at the very least, you could say that these organizations regulate and set rules while private firms and individuals are still free to act as they wish within these rules.

When a legal food product is sold, there are requirements for the maker to list ingredients and nutrition information. This lets any consumer know exactly what is in their food. But when a product is illegal, the requirements to list ingredients becomes moot. There is certainly no reason for a maker of street drugs to put a nutrition fact label on his product. This lack of information can lead to goods that are extremely variable from seller to seller, and possibly even inconsistent from the same seller at different times. Ingredients may be unknown or even dangerous to the buyer. For example, cocaine and other street drugs may be "cut" with tiny amounts of flour, laundry detergent, or talc to slightly bulk up the weight of the product. The buyer will likely not complain to the authorities about the missing nutrition label on his drug purchase or the fact that the seller sold him a bad batch with sub-par ingredients.

The black market nature of the drugs makes the purchase more dangerous for the consumer as he will have less information about the nature of good. In addition, the black market makes the transaction itself more dangerous for both the buyer and seller since there is more likely to be violence or theft.

In legal marijuana markets, particularly in stores where THC is mixed into foods or candies, more transparency is required of the seller. There are legal requirements for labeling, packaging, and selling the product. This makes the product safer and more consistent for buyers.

What about prostitution? Prostitution is an interesting case since laws vary so widely throughout the world. In fact, it may be the activity with the biggest differences in laws from country to country.

> Making an activity illegal doesn't protect the participants. In fact, it likely makes the activity even more dangerous.

Prostitution is illegal in the United States (except in Nevada), but that stance isn't shared by many countries. Prostitution is illegal in Russia, the Middle East, most parts of east Asia and in about half of the countries in Africa. But in other countries, it is either legal, decriminalized, or not regulated. However, many countries where the sex trade is legal have still outlawed *organized* prostitution, including brothels and pimping. In Canada and some Scandinavian countries, it is legal to sell sex but illegal to buy sex (try figuring that one out). That means that if a prostitute and a client get caught, the client is charged with a crime, but the prostitute isn't.

Laws that push prostitution underground endanger the market participants, particularly the prostitutes. If they are abused or victimized, they often have little or no recourse, and may be afraid to go to the police since they themselves were doing something illegal. This in turn means that clients, pimps, and brothel operators are more likely to get violent with the prostitutes or steal from them since it is less likely to be reported.

There is certainly an increased risk to the clients of illegal prostitution as well, in the form of STDs. In many states, you could face a civil suit if you knowingly have an STD, fail to inform your partner, and your partner contracts the disease. But men who contract a disease from a prostitute may be less likely to report the incident. The prostitute may have less of an incentive to tell the client since she still wants to get paid. There are generally no laws obligating people to disclose their STD status, but it is illegal to knowingly and recklessly transmit an STD.

Legalizing prostitution would reduce (or possibly eliminate) many of these dangers. Allowing the activity to occur "above ground" will certainly reduce violence, theft, and dangers, as victims would have a better chance at justice. Victims will report the crimes, and police will be more likely to pursue the case if a person was wronged doing a legal activity. Regulation could also come with this legality and would likely improve pay and working conditions for the prostitutes.

Even making the activity legal without heavy regulations will likely improve the conditions of the market for buyers and sellers. In Nevada, condoms are tax deductible as a work expense for prostitutes. This makes it more likely that prostitutes will engage in safer sex practices, benefitting themselves and the clients. Advertising expenses, hotels, and phone bills are deductible as well. This all helps make the "business" more legitimate and safe.

You could summarize so far as follows: Making a good or activity illegal may reduce consumption but will certainly not eliminate consumption. And those that consume via the black market face dangers which could be reduced by legal markets. Since the activity is likely to occur anyway, legalizing it seems like a way to improve the safety and well-being of participants.

Even if you don't care about drug dealers, prostitutes, or their clients, or if you have moral beliefs against these activities, we can still consider another large economic benefit of legalization: tax revenues.

A very large benefit of legalizing more activities is that we can then generate tax revenue from the sale of those activities. If people have an inelastic demand for marijuana (and it appears that they do), high taxes could be placed on it without causing large reductions in consumption, and big tax revenues could be generated. Thus, we go from marijuana and the war on drugs costing us a lot of money to marijuana generating a lot of money. This seems like a win-win scenario. The state of Colorado reports that as of late 2018, it earns over $20 million per month on marijuana tax revenues. That figure is huge, and it doesn't even include money that is saved from not having to police and prosecute people that would previously been arrested simply for ownership of cannabis.

When I was younger, I remember very few states having lotteries. In fact, 30 of the states that currently have lotteries started them after the year 1980. Much of the country saw lotteries as immoral. But when non-lottery states saw how much money other states were generating from lottery revenues, they

> Legalizing marijuana and prostitution will result in the goods and services becoming safer to trade and consume and will decrease costs of policing. Taxing these markets will lead to large revenues for public coffers.

started joining in on the action. Policy makers got tired of seeing residents driving across state borders to spend money on lotteries elsewhere. People drive across state lines to get goods that aren't legal in their state but are available in the next state. This happens with marijuana, lotteries, and even fireworks. And when this occurs, other states get money instead of your home state.

As of this writing in late 2018, 44 states currently have lotteries (Mississippi recently passed legislation approving lotteries, but they have not yet started in the state). An interesting fact is that while it allows prostitution, Nevada doesn't have state lotteries. This is not for moral reasons, but because there is a strong lobby in Nevada against lotteries for fear they would compete with casinos and other gambling revenues.

Maybe our beliefs are changing. Maybe people and politicians that were previously opposed to lotteries and marijuana for any number of moral reasons have since changed their minds. Or perhaps instead, we just place a dollar value on our morals. And at some point, the amount of money our collective moral beliefs cause us to forego becomes too much.

Our morals may guide our beliefs and behavior. But even our morals have a price tag. If the price of moral enforcement becomes to great, we may just change our morals.

The economics of this is that we should let people make their own decisions. Rather than having the government decide what should be legal, let people decide what activities they want to do. The most extreme form of this would be to legalize most (or all) activities, as long as they don't directly harm third parties.

Thus, if the individual decision maker absorbs all the possible costs and risks of the activity, we should legalize it, and let the people make their own choices. This is what economic freedom looks like.

Old People are an Expensive Problem

According to folklore, Eskimos put old people on ice floes and set them adrift in the ocean. This action was either assisted suicide or involuntary senilicide.

According to the 90s TV show *Dinosaurs* in an episode titled "Hurling Day", it was a tradition for families to throw elders into a tar pit on their 72nd birthday.

The rationale for doing these actions was to eliminate citizens who had become a burden or a drain on their families and society.

Certainly, no one would seriously suggest hurling our elders into a tar pit. But old people today are becoming problematic in a sense – they are very expensive. This expense is almost entirely due to health care costs, and it results in the rest of us paying higher insurance premiums and taxes.

+++++++++++++

Researchers generally conclude that the Eskimo folklore is somewhat true, but also somewhat exaggerated. The elimination of old people was rare, but not unheard of, and usually occurred during famines. There are documented cases of senilicide, but the method of death was usually not sending them on an ice floe into the sea.

This may sound heartless, and maybe it is. The Eskimos were doing a very difficult cost-benefit analysis. When food ran short, the group had to make decisions about who to feed and who not to feed. They decided that long-term chance of survival was the determining factor, so the elderly were the first to go.

No matter how much truth or fiction there is to the Eskimo stories, our concerns about the elderly of today arise for a different reason: health care costs.

Health care follows the well-known 80-20 rule. (If you've never heard of the 80-20 rule, look it up online and read about it. It is fascinating how many places it shows up). In health care, 80% of the expenditures in the United States are incurred by just 20% of the population. In this same vein, just 5% of the of the population incurs 50% of all health care expenses. For most of our lives, we are in the 95% of the population that isn't very expensive in terms of health care provision. But when we get old, our health care expenses grow very large and very fast.

Consider the following numbers:

- Health care spending (public and private combined) makes up almost 20% of our GDP
- Medicare and Medicaid make up over 20% of all government spending
- 80-year-olds have a 35% chance of surgery in their last year

Here are some numbers specific to Medicare:

- 30% is spent on people who are in the last year of their life
- 20% of recipients have surgery in their final month of life
- 10% of recipients have surgery in their final week of life

Examining these numbers, a quick back-of-the-napkin calculation estimates that as much as 8% of government spending is allocated to people in the last year of their life. Our government spends a huge amount of money on health care, and a very large and disproportionate amount of that spending goes to very old people, who are often very close to death.

Few would argue that this medical spending is necessary for the old people. But we can question the benefits received. Is it worth spending tens of thousands of dollars (surgery, recovery, hospital stay, medicine, physical therapy) on someone who is only giving to live for one more month? Or one more week?

Health care is subject to diminishing returns. At first, surgery, medicine, doctors, and nurses can greatly improve the health and quality of life for a patient. But after a while, the patient will be spending a lot of money and not getting much in return. And this spending will likely be done

By some estimates, we can conclude that up to 8% of all government spending is allocated to people in the last year of their life. Is this a desirable or sustainable distribution of spending?

through insurance companies or government programs. So in the end, all of us pay for it, either through higher insurance premiums or higher taxes. Is it worth it to pay for extremely expensive health care that simply results in the patient living for a short while longer with a very low quality of life with drugs, pain, and machines, all while in a hospital?

Should we be more willing to "accept" death? Should we focus more on palliative care rather than aggressive and expensive interventions that may simply prolong a low-quality life?

These are tough questions to ask, so they often go unasked. But if we really want to try to tackle the issue of health care costs, it's a topic we cannot avoid.

At this point, many people would chime in and suggest there are other ways to reduce the costs of health care without sacrificing quality of care, quantity of care, or tossing old people into tar pits. Some want to have more socialized health care, or promote a "Medicare for All" plan, stating that it will reduce costs. Some of these plans may be projected to reduce costs, but they will also reduce quality and quantity of care. No matter what method of health care delivery we choose, health care is still limited. It is finite. It is scarce. And governments cannot eliminate scarcity. In countries where the government is the provider of most health care, costs are kept down by limiting what drugs and services are available. In other words, the government has the right to decline health care by calling your needs "elective" or optional. Cheaper health care won't do you any good if it's cheap partly because the government won't provide care.

There are hundreds, it not thousands, of academic and research papers discussing health care issues. There are entire courses and books that discuss the subject of health care economics. But there are always tradeoffs. The typical tradeoff is choosing between expensive but readily available health care, or cheaper but limited care. Without major advancements in technology, we can't get more for cheaper. Changing who pays for the treatment won't solve scarcity and it won't solve the issue of a very small number of people using up a very large amount of health care.

Back to talking about old people now. Scarcity of health care is a problem we're not going to solve. The only question we can realistically deal with is who should get the health care we have. For example, should the donated kidney go to the 16 year old or the 85 year old? The Eskimos and fictional dinosaurs would generally opt for age-based prioritization. If enough health care is available, give it to everyone. But if there's not enough, give it to the younger people first. All other things equal, we're going to get much more bang for our buck with this allocation.

Of course, others will argue that the ability to recover and live a meaningful life should be the main criteria for health care allocation, rather than just examining age. This makes sense, but in many cases, there is just too much uncertainty. At the very least, the younger person will always have a chance at many more years of life while the older patient will not.

The reality of our elderly problem will become even more obvious in the next few years. The United States is getting older on average. This is because of the Baby Boomer generation aging well into their 70s currently, while generations after that time period had fewer kids. This problem will affect health care spending as well as social security. There is a big, expensive, gray train heading toward us, and we don't really have any solutions in hand yet.

Health care is paid for differently than other goods. Much of it is paid for through insurance companies or government programs such as Medicare and Medicaid. When that occurs, we ultimately have a system in which a large number of young and healthy people are paying premiums and/or taxes that subsidize the very old and sick people. From the numbers given earlier, you could say that 95% of the people are subsidizing the 5% of people who use an extremely disproportionate amount of health care. That's just the nature of how insurance works. Everybody pays in, but most people don't take out. But the few that *do* take money out tend to take out a lot to pay for large expenses.

"Medicare for All" would still be very expensive to administer. It wouldn't solve our health care cost problem, it would just change how we pay for it.

It's important to note that a "Medicare for All" system would <u>not</u> change this dynamic. It would just have the dynamic operated through the government rather than private insurance companies. Large tax increases would be necessary for this funding. And these would not be just taxes on the wealthiest people – everyone from the middle class and upward would see large tax hikes to fund this project. As an example, many European countries with a more socialist-style health care system have marginal tax rates above 50% which begin at income levels of about $50,000 per year. In other words, the median family is giving up about half of their earnings at the dollar to fund these programs. The "Medicare for All" idea is gaining momentum in the United States, but there will certainly be backlash if it is ever adopted and people see how costly it really is after they examine the taxes coming out of their paychecks to cover the expenses.

Another reason that "Medicare for All" could be problematic is that it puts government in charge of almost all health care. Health care is a large part of our lives, and this would necessitate a huge increase in the size and scope of government. A very real concern about this is that the government would ultimately decide which treatments are given to the people (whether you're old or not). When a central authority determines allocation, we usually get a less-than-stellar result. This is why there are often long waits for health care in other countries – the government isn't efficient at determining what people need. In addition, costs are kept down by limiting health care availability, so wait times increase. And in the worst scenarios, the government will simply decide it won't pay for or provide the care you need.

Consider the case of Alfie Evans, a boy born in England in 2016. He was diagnosed with a degenerative neurological condition, and there were fights between Alfie's parents and the British NHS (National Health Service) over his treatment. The NHS was going to stop treating Alfie, which would result in his death. A hospital in Rome said that it would care for Alfie with some surgeries and other treatments to keep him alive in hopes that his conditions would improve. However, the NHS refused to allow Alfie to leave the country and be transferred to the Italian hospital, and he ultimately died. This should strike you as absolutely terrifying – the government wouldn't allow the family to leave the country so their boy could get treated elsewhere. This isn't a case about sanctity of life, religion, or political beliefs. It's an illustration of the dangers of extreme

> When the government pays for the care, the government will decide what care you get.

government overreach, in which the government decided the life and death fate of a child against his parent's wishes. With a single distributor of all health care, the family had no other options.

You could argue that a private insurance company may stop paying for treatment as well. But a private company could never prevent you from leaving the country to seek treatment elsewhere. They could never prevent you from working with another insurance company, another hospital, or a charity to pay for the treatment.

This case illustrates not only a very troubling example of extreme government intervention into the lives of citizens, but the broader issue of how we pay for and distribute health care. When we as individuals don't pay for our own health care, we eventually lose the ability to choose what care we receive. When a private insurance company or a government program pays our health care bills, they will ultimately start having a larger and larger say in what types of care get covered. The entity paying the health care bill becomes the one who has the power to decide what care is given. This is what's known as the principal-agent problem. The person paying for the care is not the one who is receiving it, and the payer and the recipient have their own incentives as well as conflicting views of what is needed.

The issue of insurance and health care will continue to be a murky and complicated issue for decades to come, especially as our society continues to age. But keep in mind that a "Medicare for All" structure is not a panacea to our current problems. Real solutions will need to come to terms with this and realize that we may not be able to give everyone all the health care they want for a low price and low taxes. There are always tradeoffs.

9 780359 209262